Miss Hughes.

CW01666207

Internet Challenges

Written by

Terry Johnson

0540C

Prim-Ed Publishing

FOREWORD

Children generally love to surf the Net and it has fast become the number-one source of reference when searching for information. However, the two don't necessarily combine to produce the required results. Children often spend many minutes trying to locate information on the Net, which may have been located in just a few minutes via other resources.

One of the reasons for this is that children, and many adults, have not yet developed the skills needed to 'fine-tune' their research, with frustration often being the end result. The aim of this book is to develop those skills in a fun and interesting way so that the time taken to find the information they are seeking is dramatically reduced. This book not only captures and stimulates the children's interest, but improves their Internet research skills dramatically!

The teacher's role throughout these activities is twofold—firstly, creating the forum for the children to discuss, analyse and improve the search pathways they select and, secondly, in questioning the validity of information those pathways offer.

Each book is divided into three sections:

- The first focuses on children developing an awareness that keywords and phrases used to search the Internet can affect the pathway taken to find the answer.
- The second section focuses on several questions on a theme, with class discussion invited for children to support their found answers and evaluate the authenticity of the website.
- The final section requires children to make more detailed notes on a topic, which will then be used to put together a presentation in the form of a project at the end of the section. Curriculum links, answers and web addresses (URLs) for the questions have also been provided.

CONTENTS

Internet websites

In some cases, websites or specific URLs may be recommended. While these are checked and rechecked at the time of publication, the publisher has no control over any subsequent changes which may be made to webpages. It is strongly recommended that the class teacher checks all URLs before allowing children to access them.

View all pages online

http://www.prim-ed.com

Section A: Pathways

In this section, children are required to research the Internet to find answers to specific questions. As they research, they are required to record the pathway taken. A pathway simply means the route or path taken to arrive at the answer. This will be determined by the words used as search words and the websites entered.

There may be more than one correct pathway—children may find completely different pathways, yet end up with the same answer. On the other hand, a different pathway may result in finding a completely different answer. For example, to the question, 'Which is the world's largest city?', children could end up with many different answers, depending on the path taken.

These activities are designed so children can focus on developing an accurate and repeatable method of Internet research.

Activities 3, 6, 9 and 12 do not have the same focus. In these activities the emphasis is on speed. Children do not need to record how they arrived at the answer—just the answer itself and the time taken to find it.

Pathways

- Keywords are fundamental to selecting a good pathway. Children will pick up this concept quickly but some preliminary work is certainly beneficial. A good starting question is, 'Which film has seen the largest assembly of animals for any film?' At the same time, look at the different pathways taken through even minor changes, such as making a word plural or singular. For example, do you arrive at the same pathway if your keyword is 'animal' instead of 'animals?'
- Many people believe that the syntax of the keywords can also affect the pathway, so allow children to practise changing the order of keywords, or adding/subtracting signs such as the addition sign, so they can work out for themselves what is needed and what is not.
- Synonyms also play an important role in locating the best pathway. For example, the question, 'Which theme park attracts the largest number of visitors per year?' could also be worded, 'Which amusement park draws the highest total of people annually?' Changing just one word can alter a pathway for the better, so extending vocabulary is paramount.
- Follow-up work is essential. Children must be given the chance to compare answers and the pathways taken to arrive at the answer.

Critical questioning

Regardless of the skills that a researcher may or may not have, there are many traps he/she needs to be aware of when surfing the Net for the most accurate information. Critical questions which need to be asked include:

- How relevant is the site to my research?
- How accurate is the information?
- Is there evidence to support the claim?
- Is the site up to date?
- Was the information correct at one time but incorrect now?
- Is the view biased?
- What are the consequences of believing all that is presented?

By the end of this book, children should be automatically asking these critical questions themselves.

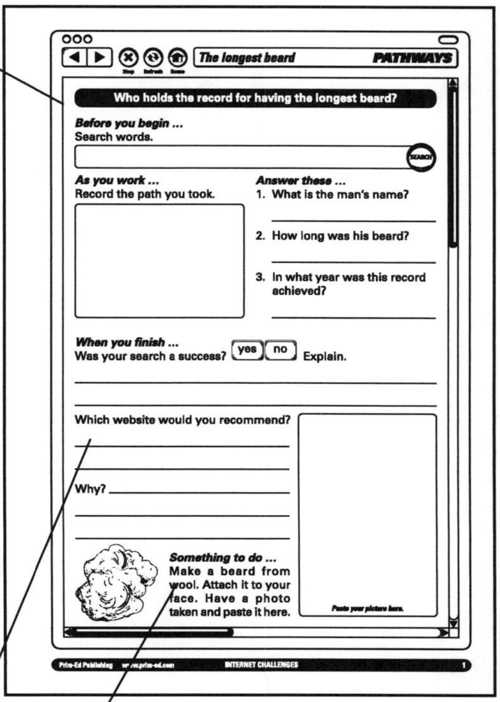
The longest beard PATHWAYS

Who holds the record for having the longest beard?

Before you begin ... Search words.

As you work ... Record the path you took.

Answer these ...
1. What is the man's name?
2. How long was his beard?
3. In what year was this record achieved?

When you finish ... Was your search a success? yes no Explain.

Which website would you recommend?

Why?

Something to do ... Make a beard from wool. Attach it to your face. Have a photo taken and paste it here.

Paste your picture here.

Prim-Ed Publishing www.prim-ed.com INTERNET CHALLENGES 1

The most enjoyable aspect of these activities is undoubtedly allowing the children to test for themselves the information they have obtained. Give them the opportunity to:

- make a beard equalling the longest ever,
- make a paper aeroplane and record the time it spends aloft,
- hold a survey in your community to see who the tallest woman is and draw comparisons,
- use mathematical concepts to make their own smallest nightclub, or
- graph the increase in speed from the invention of the car to the present.

The options are innumerable!

Section B: Researching themes

In each activity in this section, children will be required to research the Internet to find the answers to questions on a common theme.

When all children have completed their research, the class needs to discuss the answers. Children can record discussion notes in the space provided. In most instances, you can assume that if the vast majority of children have the same answer, that is the correct one. However, children who do have alternative answers should have the opportunity to debate their answer if they feel convinced there was an oversight by the majority.

For those who are brave enough, another challenge has also been set—a further question more difficult than the previous ones.

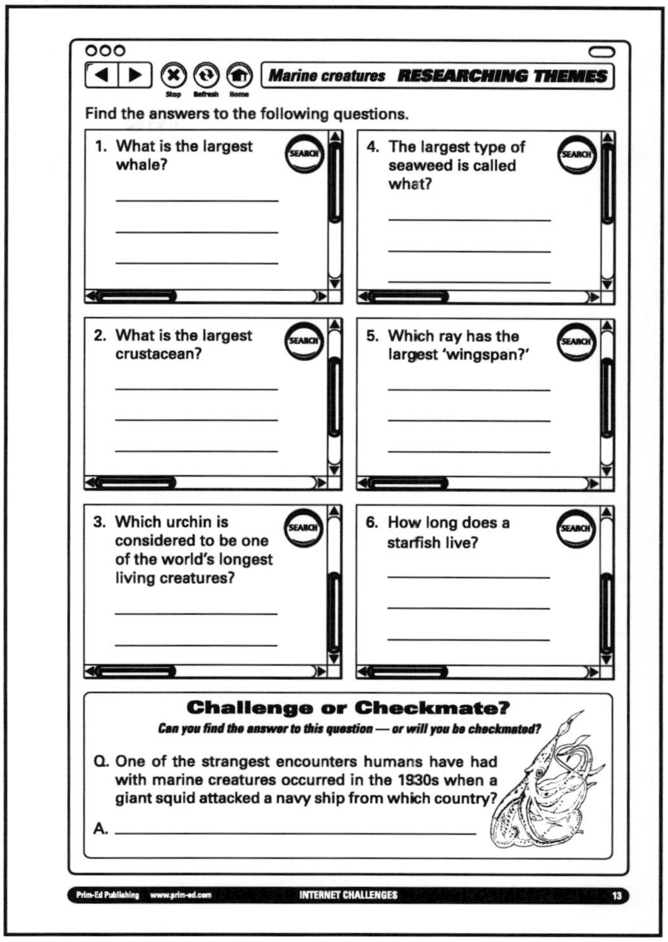
Stop Refresh Home Marine creatures RESEARCHING THEMES

Find the answers to the following questions.

1. What is the largest whale?
2. What is the largest crustacean?
3. Which urchin is considered to be one of the world's longest living creatures?
4. The largest type of seaweed is called what?
5. Which ray has the largest 'wingspan?'
6. How long does a starfish live?

Challenge or Checkmate?

Can you find the answer to this question — or will you be checkmated?

Q. One of the strangest encounters humans have had with marine creatures occurred in the 1930s when a giant squid attacked a navy ship from which country?

A.

Prim-Ed Publishing www.prim-ed.com INTERNET CHALLENGES 13

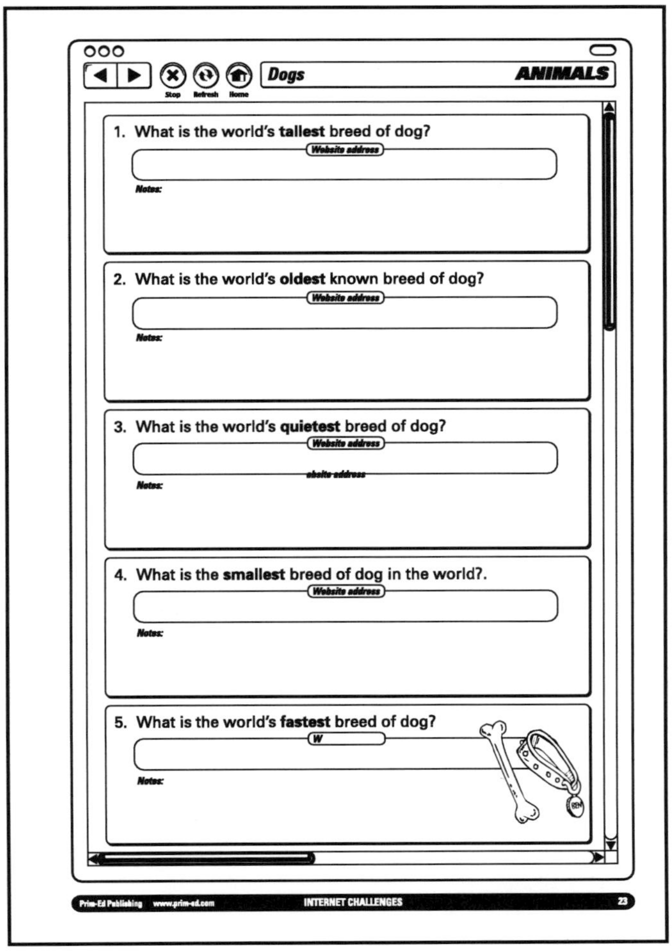
Stop Refresh Home Dogs ANIMALS

1. What is the world's **tallest** breed of dog?
Website address
Notes:
2. What is the world's **oldest** known breed of dog?
Website address
Notes:
3. What is the world's **quietest** breed of dog?
Website address
Notes:
4. What is the **smallest** breed of dog in the world?.
Website address
Notes:
5. What is the world's **fastest** breed of dog?
W
Notes:

Prim-Ed Publishing www.prim-ed.com INTERNET CHALLENGES 23

Section C: Animals

In this section, children will be required to research and find answers, as in Sections A and B. This time, however, children will be required to record the web address used as well as make additional notes. For example, if asked to find which bird builds the largest nest, it is necessary to not just write the name of the bird, but to add some additional details as well. Additional details may include:

- how big the nest can be,
- what materials the bird uses, and
- where these birds can be found.

These notes will be valuable to children later when completing the project at the end of this section.

Country	Subject	Strand/Unit	Level	Objectives
England	ICT	Finding things out Reviewing ... Breadth of study	KS2	• 1a – talk about what information they need and how they can find and use it • 1b – prepare information for development using ICT, including selecting suitable sources, finding information, classifying it and checking it for accuracy • 1c – interpret information, check it is relevant and reasonable and to think about what might happen if there were any errors or omissions • 4c – talk about how they could improve future work • 5a – work with a range of information to consider its characteristics and purposes • 5b – work with others to explore a variety of information sources and ICT tools
Northern Ireland	English	Reading	KS2	• search for and find information using a computer • read a range of non-fiction materials • read for information • acquire and develop skills necessary to locate information efficiently
Republic of Ireland	English	Reading (Competence) (Cognitive)	3rd/4th	• experience different types of text • develop basic information retrieval skills • use IT to increase motivation to read and to enhance reading development
Scotland	ICT	Searching and researching	C D E	• use a web browser independently • search across a range of media • use a search engine • refine searches
Wales	IT	Communicating and handling	KS2	• interpret, analyse and check the plausibility of information held on ICT systems, and select the elements required for particular purposes, considering the consequences of any errors • consider what kinds of information is needed and how they can find and use it

It is impossible to search the entire World Wide Web as there are literally billions of pages available. So, when you need to find something about a particular subject, how do you know which pages to read? Easy—you visit an Internet search engine! Search engines are special sites that help us to find information stored on other sites.

Types of search engines

Some search engines use special software 'robots' to 'crawl' or 'spider' the web. The 'spiders' take a web page's content and create key search words that enable you to find pages you are looking for.

For example, if you are looking for the highest mountain in Australia, it would be advisable to type the following words into your search query:

highest mountain Australia SEARCH

The engine will look for pages that have all three of these keywords, and then rank them by firstly taking note of the number of keywords within that page and also where the words were found. The ranking will hopefully (but not always) give you the most relevant web pages first. Google® is an example of this type of search engine.

Some search engines are more like directories that are edited by humans. If you are an author of a web page and want to get onto a directory, you can either pay to have your page viewed and listed quickly or not pay and wait several months for it to be viewed and listed. The author can nominate the keywords it wants the page to be linked to. Yahoo® is an example of this type of search engine.

Recommendations

Google® is the search engine recommended for answering the questions in this book. When trying to locate the best pages to investigate the possible answers, simply select several keywords from the question. You will find as you progress through the book you will get better and better at doing this. Then type in those keywords, with a space between them, as in the example given previously: highest mountain Australia.

You can be more precise in the way you enter keywords, thus giving you a more accurate set of pages that Google® will offer you. To learn how to do this, try reading the excellent article 'Search Engine Math' from the website <'www.searchenginewatch.com>.

It is important to note that even the slightest change in the keywords (e.g. 'world's' versus 'world') can alter the pages that Google® retrieves for you. Also note that one of Google®'s disadvantages is that if you want information about the heart, for example, then Google® will not retrieve pages that use 'cardiac' as a keyword. Hence you need to become adept at using synonyms. Instead of 'dearest', try using 'most expensive'. Instead of 'commonest', try using 'most common'.

Teachers and children should be aware that not all webpages will give the same answer. With new dinosaur bones being discovered each year, for example, some websites still claim the Sauroposeidon to be the tallest dinosaur, while others now claim the Brachiosaurus to have been taller. With astronomers discovering new moons each year, some websites claim that Saturn has the largest number of moons, while others now suggest Jupiter has overtaken it. Google® does not have the ability to eliminate webpages which make false, outrageous, biased or out-of-date claims.

Complete the following checklist to evaluate a selected website.

1. Web address of site.

Address:	**http://**	**▶ go**

2. Why did you decide to use this site?

3. Who has the copyright to the site?

©

4. When was the information posted or last updated?

5. Rate the navigation of the site.

1 2 3 4 5 6 7 8 9 10

Difficult **Easy**

6. Rate the appearance of the site.

1 2 3 4 5 6 7 8 9 10

Awful! **Awesome!**

7. Is the information on the site reliable? yes no

How do you know?

8. Would you recommend the site to others? yes no

Why/Why not?

Stop Refresh Home

The longest beard

PATHWAYS

Who holds the record for having the longest beard?

Before you begin ...
Search words.

SEARCH

As you work ...
Record the path you took.

Answer these ...

1. What is the man's name?

____

2. How long was his beard?

____

3. In what year was this record achieved?

____

When you finish ...
Was your search a success? yes no Explain.

____

____

Which website would you recommend?

____

Why? _______________

____

____

Something to do ...
Make a beard from wool the length of the longest beard. Attach it to your face. Have a photo taken and glue it here.

Glue your picture here.

Stop Refresh Home

Who is the richest man in the world?

Before you begin ...

Search words.

SEARCH

As you work ...

Record the path you took.

Answer these ...

1. What is his name?

2. What is his net worth?

3. How has he accumulated his wealth?

When you finish ...

Was your search a success? yes no Explain.

Which website would you recommend?

Why?

Something to do ...

Attach a picture of the richest man here.

Glue your picture here.

Find the answer to each question below and record the time taken.

QUESTIONS: **TIME:**

1. What is the biggest inland sea in the world?

2. What is the biggest insect living today?

3. The biggest gold nugget ever dug up and recorded was given what name?

4. What is the biggest lizard in the world?

5. What is the world's biggest land animal?

Which question was the easiest and fastest to answer?

What do you think were the reasons for this?

The world's tallest living tree is how tall?

Before you begin ...

Search words.

SEARCH

As you work ...

Record the path you took.

When you finish ...

Was your search a success? yes no

Explain. ______________________

____

____

In which website did you find your answer?

____

Answer these ...

1. What is the height of the tallest living tree?

____

2. What type of tree is it?

____

3. Where is the tree located?

____

4. Have there been any trees to grow taller than this tree?

____

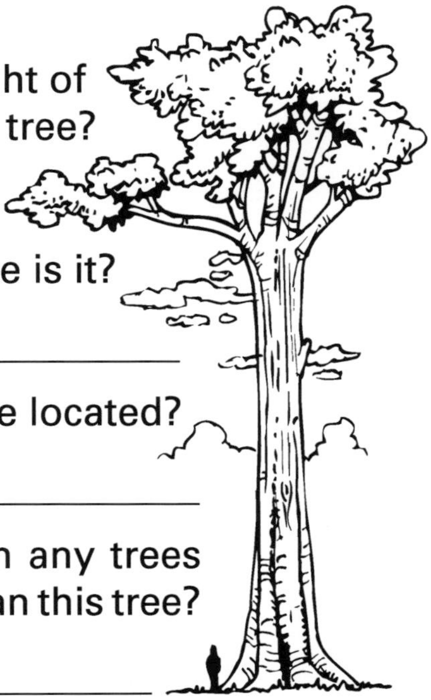

Attach a picture of the type of tree here.

What is the highest speed attained by a jet-propelled car?

Before you begin ...
Search words.

SEARCH

As you work ...
Record the path you took.

Answer these ...

1. What is the name of the car?
2. What speed did it reach?
3. Who drove the car?
4. When did it break the record to make it the fastest jet-propelled car?

When you finish ...
Was your search a success? yes no Explain.

Which website would you recommend?

Attach a picture of the car here.

Attach your picture here.

Find the answer to each question below and record the time taken.

QUESTIONS: **TIME:**

1. What is the highest mountain in Africa?

2. Which capital city is at the highest altitude above sea level?

3. What is the highest score by a team in a Test cricket innings?

4. What is the highest money-making film ever?

5. Which country had the highest consumption of tea in 1997?

Which question was the easiest and fastest to answer?

What do you think were the reasons for this?

What is the name of the world's smallest nightclub?

Before you begin ...

Search words.

SEARCH

As you work ...

Record the path you took.

When you finish ...

Was your search a success?

yes no

Explain.

Which website would you recommend?

Answer these ...

1. What is the name of the nightclub?
2. Where is the nightclub located?
3. What is the area of the nightclub?
4. How does this area compare with the area of your bedroom?
5. How many people can attend the club at any one time?

Something to do ...

Have you ever had that many people in your bedroom at any one time? If not, try it!

Stop Refresh Home

The strongest creature **PATHWAYS**

In relation to its size, which creature is considered to be the strongest?

Before you begin ...

Predict which species of animal this creature belongs to e.g. mammal, amphibian, insect and so on.

Search words

SEARCH

As you work ...

Record the path you took.

When you finish ...

Was your search a success?

yes no

Explain.

Which website would you recommend?

Answer these ...

1. What is the name of the creature?
2. How strong is it?
3. Was your prediction correct?

Something to do ...

Attach a picture of the creature here.

Attach your picture here.

Stop Refresh Home

The busiest ... PATHWAYS

Find the answer to each question below and record the time taken.

QUESTIONS: **TIME:**

1. Which museum is considered to be the busiest in the world?

2. Which train station is the busiest in the world?

3. What is the busiest port in the world?

4. What is regarded as the busiest bridge in the world?

5. According to the Airports Council International, what was the busiest airport in the world in 2002?

Which question was the most difficult to answer?

What do you think were the reasons for this?

What is the name of the world's steepest street?

Before you begin ...
Search words.

SEARCH

As you work ...
Record the path you took.

When you finish ...
Was your search a success?

yes no

Explain.

Which website would you recommend?

Something to do ...
Attach a picture of the street here.

Answer these ...

1. What is the name of the street?
2. In which city is the street located?
3. How steep is the street?
4. A dispute has arisen about the street's true gradient. If this street is not as steep as stated, which city could then lay claim to having the world's steepest street?

Attach your picture here.

Stop Refresh Home

Smelliest bird **PATHWAYS**

What is considered to be the world's smelliest bird?

Before you begin ...

Search words.

SEARCH

As you work ...

Record the path you took.

When you finish ...

Was your search a success?

yes no

Explain.

Which website would you recommend? Why?

Answer these ...

1. What is the name of the bird?
2. What causes this bird to be so smelly?
3. Where does this bird live?

Something to do ...

Attach a picture of the bird here.

Attach your picture here.

Find the answer to each question below and record the time taken.

QUESTIONS: **TIME:**

1. What is the slowest moving land mammal?

2. What is the slowest fish?

3. Who holds the record for the slowest century in Test cricket and how long did it take?

4. What is the slowest growing flowering plant, not flowering until it is almost 150 years old?

5. What is the slowest flying bird?

Which question was the easiest and fastest to answer?

What do you think were the reasons for this?

Stop Refresh Home

Find the answers to the following questions.

1. What is the **largest** whale?

SEARCH

____

____

____

4. The **largest** type of seaweed is called what?

SEARCH

____

____

____

2. What is the **largest** crustacean?

SEARCH

____

____

____

5. Which ray has the **largest** 'wingspan'?

SEARCH

____

____

____

3. Which urchin is considered to be one of the world's **longest** living creatures?

SEARCH

____

____

6. How **long** does a starfish live?

SEARCH

____

____

____

Challenge or Checkmate?

Can you find the answer to this question — or will you be checkmated?

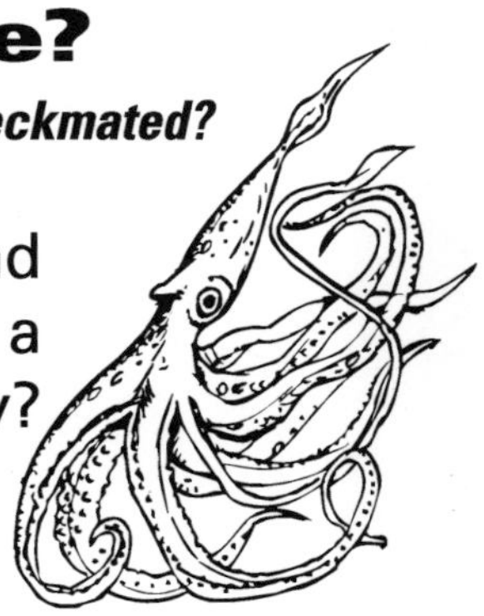

Q. One of the strangest encounters humans have had with marine creatures occurred in the 1930s when a giant squid attacked a navy ship from which country?

A. ____

Stop Refresh Home

Women — RESEARCHING THEMES

Find the answers to the following questions.

1. Who was considered to be the **richest** woman in the world in 2003, according to Forbes billionaire rankings?

   SEARCH

   ____

2. Who is recognised as being the **tallest** woman currently living?

   SEARCH

   ____

   ____

3. What is the **highest** number of parachute jumps made by a woman?

   SEARCH

   ____

   ____

4. Known as one of the **bravest** women in the USA, which lady took over her husband's work after he was assassinated in Memphis in 1968?

   SEARCH

   ____

5. Who has been the **longest** serving Queen of the United Kingdom?

   SEARCH

   ____

   ____

6. How old was the **oldest** woman when she died?

   SEARCH

   ____

   ____

Challenge or Checkmate?

Can you find the answer to this question — or will you be checkmated?

Q. Two of Elton John's greatest hits are both called *Candle in the wind.* The second was written as a tribute to Princess Diana. Who was the original hit a tribute to?

A. ____________________

Find the answers to the following questions.

1. What is the **hottest** planet?

____

____

____

2. What is the name of the **largest** known asteroid?

____

____

____

3. Who were the **earliest** astronomers?

____

____

____

4. 'Olympus Mons', the **largest** volcano in the solar system, is on which planet?

____

____

5. Which is the **densest** planet?

____

____

____

6. What was the name of the **first** manned spacecraft to return safely to earth?

____

____

Challenge or Checkmate?

Can you find the answer to this question — or will you be checkmated?

Q. An estimated 65 million years ago a meteorite collided with the earth and created one of the world's biggest craters. In which country is this crater located?

A. _______________

Find the answers to the following questions.

1. What is the record for the **highest** total of hotdogs eaten in a 12-minute period?

SEARCH

____

____

4. The **longest** duration for a paper airplane to remain aloft indoors is how many seconds?

SEARCH

____

2. What is the **highest** number of basketball 'free throws' made by an individual in a NBA game?

SEARCH

____

5. What is the **longest** time for balancing a football on one's head?

SEARCH

____

____

3. What is the **highest** number of ewes shorn in an 9-hour period?

SEARCH

____

____

6. What is the record for the **longest** solo drumming marathon?

SEARCH

____

____

Challenge or Checkmate?

Can you find the answer to this question — or will you be checkmated?

Q. The longest throw of a grape to be caught in someone's mouth measures how long?

A. ____

Find the answers to the following questions.

1. The world's **biggest** commercial jigsaw has how many pieces?

2. What is considered to be the world's **oldest** hobby according to a numismatist?

3. Collecting things is an interesting hobby. The **largest** known collection of tea-bag labels totals how many?

4. What is the **highest** price ever paid for a philatelic item?

5. A 'twitcher' is a term associated with one of the world's **quietest** hobbies. What is this hobby?

6. What are the two **oldest** toys in the world?

Challenge or Checkmate?

Can you find the answer to this question — or will you be checkmated?

Q. What is considered to be the world's longest miniature hobby railroad?

A. ______________________________

Stop Refresh Home

Find the answers to the following questions.

1. Who holds the distinction of being the world's **youngest** ever king?

SEARCH

4. Which Roman Emperor reigned for the **shortest** period of time?

SEARCH

2. Who has been the **oldest** President of the USA?

SEARCH

5. Who has been the **youngest** ever Chinese Emperor?

SEARCH

3. Who has been the **youngest** Prime Minister of Australia?

SEARCH

6. When did the **last** Czar of Russia die?

SEARCH

Challenge or Checkmate?

Can you find the answer to this question — or will you be checkmated?

Q. Which king/queen is currently the world's longest reigning monarch?

A. ______________________________

Find the answers to the following questions.

1. Which dinosaur is considered to have been the **tallest**?

____

____

____

2. Which dinosaur had the **biggest** skull?

____

____

____

3. What was the **heaviest** dinosaur?

____

____

____

4. What was the ***largest*** pterosaur, a flying reptile, which lived at the same time as the dinosaurs?

____

5. Which dinosaur had the **longest** name?

____

____

____

6. How big is the **biggest** dinosaur footprint?

____

____

____

Challenge or Checkmate?

Can you find the answer to this question — or will you be checkmated?

Q. What is the name of the oldest dinosaur ever found and where was it discovered?

A. ____

Find the answers to the following questions.

1. What is the **fastest** flying insect?

4. Which species of butterfly has the **longest** known migration?

2. What was the **biggest** insect to have ever lived?

5. Which order of insects has the **largest** number of species?

3. What is the world's **heaviest** insect?

6. How **many** eggs can a queen bee lay in one day?

Challenge or Checkmate?

Can you find the answer to this question — or will you be checkmated?

Q. Which insect created the greatest concentration of animals the world has ever witnessed?

A. ______________________________

Find the answers to the following questions.

1. What is the **largest** organ of the human body?

SEARCH

2. What is the human body's **longest** bone?

SEARCH

3. What is the **most common** blood group?

SEARCH

4. Where in the body is the skin the **thickest**?

SEARCH

5. What is the **biggest** muscle of the human body?

SEARCH

6. How **long** is the large intestine when stretched out?

SEARCH

Challenge or Checkmate?

Can you find the answer to this question — or will you be checkmated?

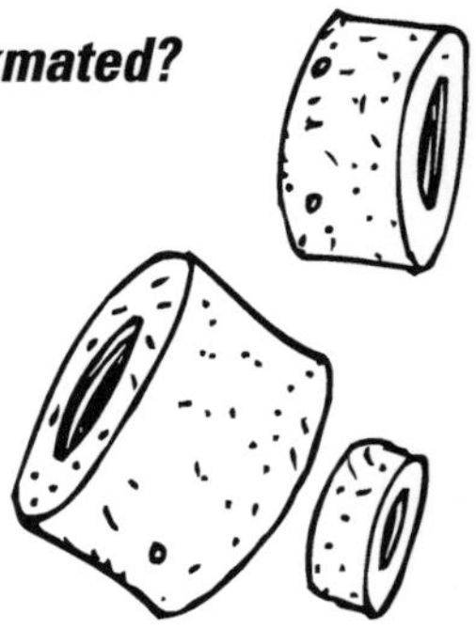

Q. What are the smallest blood vessels called?

A. ______________________

Find the answers to the following questions.

1. What is the **longest** steel roller-coaster in the world called?

____

____

____

4. In which country is the world's **oldest** operating theme park?

____

____

2. In which city is the world's **tallest** Ferris wheel located?

____

____

____

5. One of the world's **biggest** and **fastest** roller-coasters can be found at Cedar Point Theme Park in Ohio, USA. What is it called?

____

3. What is the world's **fastest** free fall speed slide called?

____

____

____

6. Where has the **newest** theme park been built?

____

____

____

Challenge or Checkmate?

Can you find the answer to this question — or will you be checkmated?

Q. The world's tallest wooden roller-coaster is how high?

A. _______________

Stop Refresh Home

Dogs

ANIMALS

1. What is the world's **tallest** breed of dog?

Website address

Notes:

2. What is the world's **oldest** known breed of dog?

Website address

Notes:

3. What is the world's **quietest** breed of dog?

Website address

Notes:

4. What is the **smallest** breed of dog in the world?.

Website address

Notes:

5. What is the world's **fastest** breed of dog?

Website address

Notes:

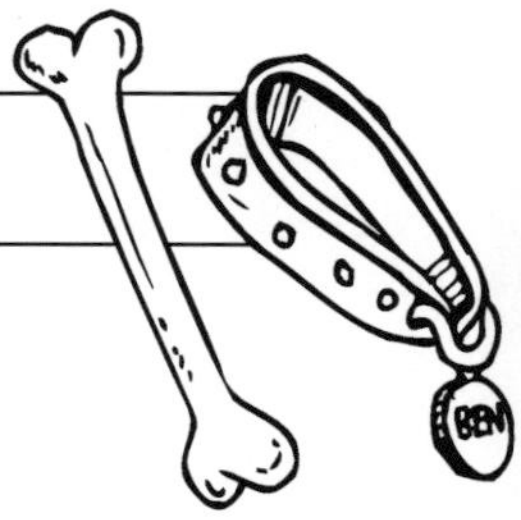

Stop Refresh Home

Cats

ANIMALS

1. What is the **biggest** cat species?

Website address

Notes:

2. The **dearest** domestic cat ever bought cost how much?

Website address

Notes:

3. What is the world record for the **longest** cat's whiskers?

Website address

Notes:

4. What is the **largest** burial site of cats?

Website address

Notes:

5. What is the **largest** litter of kittens on record? How many survived?

Website address

Notes:

1. Which bird has the **fastest** wing beat?

Website address

Notes:

2. Which bird has the **longest** wingspan?

Website address

Notes:

3. Which bird builds the **largest** nests?

Website address

Notes:

4. What is the **highest** flying bird in the world?

Website address

Notes:

5. Which bird lays the **largest** eggs?

Website address

Notes:

1. What is the world's **biggest** freshwater fish?

Website address

Notes:

2. What is the world's **largest** fish?

Website address

Notes:

3. What is considered to be South America's **deadliest** and **fiercest** fish?

Website address

Notes:

4. Which fish holds the record for being the world's **heaviest** bony fish?

Website address

Notes:

5. What is the world's **deadliest** stinging fish according to the toxic levels of its poison?

Website address

Notes:

Stop Refresh Home

Bears **ANIMALS**

1. What is the **largest** brown bear?

Website address

Notes:

2. What is the **smallest** bear?

Website address

Notes:

3. Which bear is considered to be the world's **largest** land carnivore?

Website address

Notes:

4. Which South American bear is one of the **rarest** of all bears?

Website address

Notes:

5. The cubs of which bear are the smallest of any newborn mammals (excluding marsupials)?

Website address

Notes:

Stop Refresh Home

Horses

1. What is the **smallest** breed of horse?

Website address

Notes:

2. Which breed of horse is considered to be the **oldest** and **purest**?

Website address

Notes:

3. What is the **fastest** of all horse breeds taking into consideration both speed and endurance?

Website address

Notes:

4. What is the **biggest** breed of horse?

Website address

Notes:

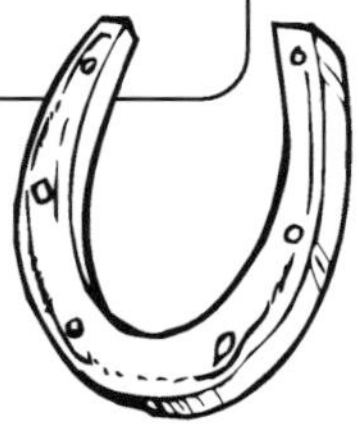

5. Which is not only the **largest** and **hairiest**, but also the most endangered species of donkey?

Website address

Notes:

Stop Refresh Home

Snakes

ANIMALS

1. What type of snake is the world's **longest**?

Website address

Notes:

2. What type of snake is generally regarded as being the world's **heaviest** snake?

Website address

Notes:

3. Which Australian snake is the world's **deadliest** land snake?

Website address

Notes:

4. What is the length of the **longest** snake ever recorded?

Website address

Notes:

5. What is the world's **deadliest** sea snake?

Website address

Notes:

1. What is the **deadliest** frog?

Website address

Notes:

2. What is the **longest** recorded jump by a frog?

Website address

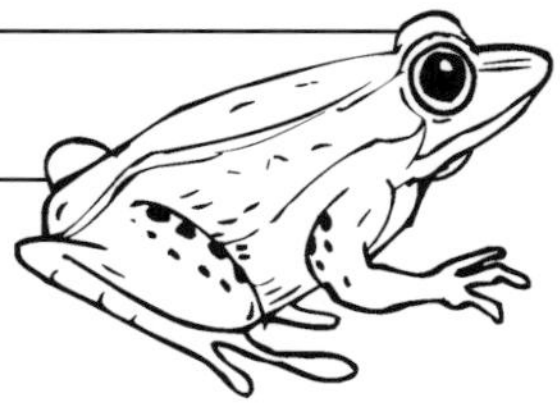

Notes:

3. What is the name of one of the two frogs which vie for the distinction of being the world's **smallest** frog?

Website address

Notes:

4. What is the **biggest** frog in the world?

Website address

Notes:

5. One of the **strangest** frogs — it actually lives in a desert — is called the Catholic frog. In which country can you find this frog?

Website address

Notes:

1. What is the **biggest** great ape?

Website address

Notes:

2. Which one of the four kinds of great apes is the **smallest**?

Website address

Notes:

3. Which great ape is considered to be the world's **largest** arboreal animal?

Website address

Notes:

4. Which great ape is the **loneliest** due to its solitary nature?

Website address

Notes:

5. Is the boss of the chimpanzee community, called the alpha male, usually the **smartest** male or the **biggest** male?

Website address

Notes:

1. What is the **largest** breed of rabbit?

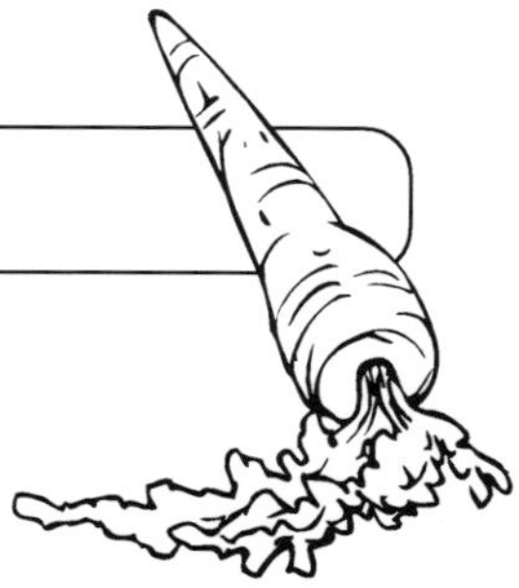

Website address

Notes:

2. Which breed of rabbit is not only one of the **rarest** but also one of the **smallest** breeds?

Website address

Notes:

3. Rabbit meat is one of the **lowest** in cholesterol and **highest** in protein. True or false?

Website address

Notes:

4. Which breed of rabbit has the **longest** ears?

Website address

Notes:

5. Which two breeds are considered to be the **smallest** breeds of rabbit?

Website address

Notes:

TASK

You are required to design a PowerPoint® presentation of at least 20 slides.

CONTENT

Part A

Choose from **one** of these options:

1. Select the 15 questions that interested you the most. There does not need to be any link among the questions.
2. Select any three animals and concentrate solely on the 15 questions covered within those topics.
3. Select a common theme and use that theme to make up the 15 questions. For example, you may choose the theme 'Biggest and Smallest'.

Part B

Select one question that really interests you and extend this topic over five slides. For example, the world's deadliest frog may have captured your interest, so find out as much information as you can on this frog and organise that information into five slides.

CRITERIA

- There should be at least 10 pictures included in your PowerPoint® presentation which have been taken from websites you searched.
- You are expected to include in your slides some of the additional notes that you made.
- The emphasis for each slide should be on the information that you found while researching the question. The actual question does not have to appear on the slide.

PRESENTATION

Remember to 'Keep it Simple!' PowerPoint® presentations can sometimes include too many special effects.

AUDIENCE

Organise a parent's night, put the PowerPoint® presentations onto a big screen and let the parents see the presentations of all the class members.

SECTION A
Pathways

Longest beard .... ***page 1***

1. Hans Langseth
2. 5.33 m long
3. 1927

http://www.guinnessworldrecords.com

Richest man .... ***page 2***

1. William Gates III
2. Varies – $46.6 billion
3. Microsoft™

http://www.forbes.com

The biggest … .... ***page 3***

1. Caspian Sea
   http://www.ecoworld.org
2. Goliath Beetle
   http://www.extremescience.com
3. The Welcome Stranger (depending on definition of the term nugget)
   http://www.historyhill.com.au/Gold_ _The_Biggest_&_The_Best.html
4. Komodo Dragon
   http://www.enchantedlearning.com/subjects/reptiles/lizard/Komodoprintout.shtml
5. African Elephant
   http://www.enchantedlearning.com/subjects/mammals/elephant/Africancoloring.shtml

Tallest tree .... ***page 4***

1. 112.6 m
2. Coast Redwood (stratosphere giant)
3. Rockefeller Forest, California, USA
4. Eucalyptus tree at Mt Baw Baw, Australia measured 143 m.

http://www.guinnessworldrecords.com

Fastest car .... ***page 5***

1. Thrust Super Sonic Car
2. 1227.985 kph, 763.055 mph
3. Andy Green
4. 15/10/97

http://www.guinnessworldrecords.com

The highest .... ***page 6***

1. Mt Kilimanjaro, 5895 m
   www.globalgeografia.com/africa_eng/africa.htm
2. La Paz, Bolivia, 3632 m above sea level
   http://www.kasbah.com/guides/la_paz_editorial.htm
3. 952, Sri Lanka, 2/8/97
   http://www.cricketonly.com/cricket/DB/total/user/us03/type/T/order/D
4. Titanic (1997), $601 million
   http://www.cinemaspot.com/lists/topgrossing.htm
5. India
   http://www.tea.org.au/world/sub2.html

Smallest nightclub .... ***page 7***

1. The Minuscule of Sound
2. London, UK
3. 2.88 m^2
4. Answers will vary
5. 13 plus 1 DJ

http://www.guinnessworldrecords.com

Strongest creature .... ***page 8***

1. Rhinoceros Beetle
2. Supports up to 850 times its own weight (disputed)
3. Teacher check

http://www.extremescience.com

The busiest … .... ***page 9***

1. Air & Space Museum, Smithsonian Institution (about 9 million visitors a year)
   http://www.nasm.si.edu/events/pressroom/presskits/hazycenter/release.htm
2. Shinjuku Station, Tokyo, Japan
   http://en.wikipedia.org/wiki/Train_station
3. Singapore
   http://www.geography.about.com/cs/transportation/a/aa061603.htm
4. Howrah Bridge, Calcutta, India
   http://www.didyouknow.cd/bridges.htm
5. Hartsfield-Jackson (Atlanta)
   http://www.lostluggagetales.com/resources/airlines/busiest-airport.asp

Steepest street .... ***page 10***

1. Baldwin Street
2. Dunedin, New Zealand
3. 38°
4. San Francisco

http://www.ourshop.co.nz/baldwinstreet.htm

Smelliest bird .... ***page 11***

1. South American Hoatzin
2. Combination of diet and digestive process
3. Colombia

http://www.victorialodging.com/birding/small_big_fast_slow.htm

The slowest .... ***page 12***

1. Sloth
   http://www.hypertextbook.com/facts/1999/IvyWeinberg.shtml
2. Seahorses
   http://www.guinnessworldrecords.com
3. Mudassar Nazar, 557 minutes (1977-1978)
   http://www.cricinfo.com/db/STATS/TESTS/BATTING/SLOWEST_TEST_100S.html
4. Bolivian herb – Puya raimondii
   http://www.bbc.co.uk/nature/plants/fun/record_breakers.shtml
5. American woodcock and Eurasian woodcock (≈ 8 kph)
   http://www.birding.com/BirdRecords1.htm

SECTION B
Researching themes

Marine creatures .... ***page 13***

1. Blue whale
   http://www.enchantedlearning.com/subjects/whales/alphawhales.shtml
2. Giant Spider Crab
   http://www.oceanlink.island.net/records.html
3. Red Sea Urchin
   http://www.oregonstate.edu/dept/ncs/newsarch/2003/Nov03/urchin.htm
4. Giant Kelp
   http://www.oceanlink.island.net/records.html
5. Manta Ray
   http://www.cayman.org/fauna/manta.htm
6. On average, about 6 years.
   http://www.tanner-learning.com/questions/questions.txt

Challenge or Checkmate?

Norway

http://www.unmuseum.mus.pa.us/squid.htm

Women .... ***page 14***

1. Alice Walton
   http://www.forbes.com/2003/02/26/billionaireland.html
2. Sandy Allen
   http://www.guinnessworldrecords.com
3. 15 560, Cheryl Stearns
   http://www.guinnessworldrecords.com
4. Coretta Scott King
   http://www.galegroup.com/free_resources/whm/bio/king_c_s.htm
5. Queen Victoria, 64 years
   http://www.toursandtravel.demon.co.uk/html/victoria.htmlhtml/victoria.html
6. 122 years, 164 days
   Jeanne-Louise Calment, France
   http://www.guinessworldrecords.com

Challenge or Checkmate?

Marilyn Monroe

http://www.earfloss.com/karaoke/8900148.html

Our solar system .... ***page 15***

1. Venus
   www.physlink.com/Education/AskExperts/ae425.cfm
2. Ceres
   http://www.stardate.org/resources/ssguide/asteroids.html
3. Priests and holy men
   http://www.space.about.com/cs/astronomy101/a/astro101b.htm

4. Mars
http://www.mimp.mems.cmu.edu/~ordofmag/olymmons.htm
5. Earth
http://www.enchantedlearning.com/subjects/astronomy/planets/
6. 1961, April, Vostok 1 is launched by USSR carrying cosmonaut Yuri A. Gagarin.
http://www.aerospaceguide.net/humansinspace/vostok.html

Challenge or Checkmate?
Mexico
http://www.pip.com.au/~paceman/THE%20DINOSAUR%20KILLER.html

Unusual records .... page 16

1. 50
http://www.cnn.com/2001/US/07/04/hotdog.contest/
2. 28, Wilt Chamberlain/Adrian Dantley
http://www.nba.com/history/records/regular_freethrows.htm
3. 720. Darin Forde, NZ
http://www.shearingworld.com/records/darin_forde/darin_forde.htm
4. 27.6 sec
http://www.news.bbc.co.uk/cbbcnews/hi/sci_tech/newsid_1989000/1989676.stm
5. 2 hours
http://www.recordholders.org/en/records/ball-head.html
6. 58 hours, 17 minutes
http://www.guinessworldrecords.com

Challenge or Checkmate?
99.82 metres
http://www.guinnessworldrecords.com/

Hobbies .... page 17

1. 18 000 pieces
http://www.guinessworldrecords.com
2. Coin collecting
http://www.money.org/ynancient.html
3. 10 400 (July 2002)
http://www.felix-rotter.de/txten.htm
4. $3.8 million
http://www.coins.about.com/library/weekly/aa123102a.htm
5. Birdwatching
http://www.geocities.com/RainForest/Vines/4074/3twitch.htm
6. (i) doll (ii) yo-yo
http://www.thelittlewoodshop.co.uk/toy-trivia.php

Challenge or Checkmate?
Train Mountain Railroad Museum
http://www.trainmountain.org/

World leaders .... page 18

1. King Oyo Nyimba
http://www.denvergov.org/newsarticle.asp?id=4059
2. Ronald Reagan
http://www.ipl.org/div/farq/POTUSFARQ.html#question1
3. John (Chris) Watson
http://www.primeministers.naa.gov.au/meetpm.asp?pmId=1&pageName=inoffice
4. Otho, 90 days
http://www.ancient-treasure.com/rulers.html
5. Emperor Pu Yi
http://www.library.thinkquest.org/27629/chronicle/1908.html?tqskip1=1
6. Czar Nicholas Romanu II and his family were executed in 16 July, 1918.
http://www.hut.fi/u/milla/e/505/czar/czar7.html

Challenge or Checkmate?
King of Thailand
http://www.thailandlife.com/worldrecord.html

Dinosaurs .... page 19

1. Brachiosaurus (disputed)
http://www.kidzworld.com/site/p730.htm
2. Torosaurus
http://www.abc.net.au/dinosaurs/chronology/65/making65_2.htm
3. Argentinosaurus
www.dinodatabase.com/dinorcds03.asp
4. Quetzalcoatlus
http://www.ucmp.berkeley.edu/diapsids/pterosauria.html
5. Micropachycephalosaurus
http://www.dinodatabase.com/dinorcds04.asp
6. 1.5 metres long by 1.2 metres wide (disputed)
http://www.fpeng.peopledaily.com.cn/200103/20/eng20010320_65434.html

Challenge or Checkmate?
Prosauropod, Madagascar, 230 million years
http://www.enchantedlearning.com/subjects/dinosaurs/questions/faq/Oldest.shtml

Insects .... page 20

1. Dragonfly
http://www.newsday.com/other/special/naturalworld/ny-nw-insects.story
2. Ancient Dragonfly (Meganeura)
http://www.uky.edu/Agriculture/Entomology/ythfacts/bugfun/trivia.htm
3. Goliath beetle
http://www.indianchild.com/insect_facts.htm
4. Monarch
http://www.bbg.org/gar2/topics/wildlife/handbooks/butterflyguide/3.html
5. Beetles (Coleoptera)
http://www.earthlife.net/insects/six01.html
6. up to 2000 per day
http://en.wikipedia.org/wiki/Queen_bee

Challenge or Checkmate?
Locust
http://www.denver-rmn.com/millennium/0622mile.shtml

The human body .... page 21

1. Skin
http://www.bbc.co.uk/science/humanbody/body/factfiles/skin/skin.shtml
2. Femur (Thighbone)
http://www.bbc.co.uk/science/humanbody/body/factfiles/leg/leg_and_foot.shtml
3. Group O
http://www.blood.co.uk/pages/secrets_in_blood.html
4. Soles of feet (and palms)
http://www.kidshealth.org/parent/general/body_basics/skin_hair_nails.html
5. Gluteus maximus (buttocks)
http://www.investigator.org.au/grossOut.htm
6. 1.5 metres
http://hypertextbook.com/facts/2001/AnneMarieThomesino.html

Challenge or Checkmate?
Capillaries
http://www.greenfield.fortunecity.com/rattler/46/bvintro.htm

Theme parks .... page 22

1. Steel Dragon 2000, Nagashima, 2479 m
http://www.ultimaterollercoaster.com/coasters/records/
2. Osaka, Japan
http://www.jinjapan.org/kidsweb/news/97-8/wheel.html
3. Summit Plummet
http://www.wdisneyw.co.uk/bb.html
4. Denmark, opened 1583
http://www.napha.org/history.html
5. Top Thrill Dragster
http://www.cedarpoint.com/ttd/
6. Euro Disneyland, 1992 (may vary)
http://www.library.thinkquest.org/27629/chronicle/1908.html?tqskip1=1

Challenge or Checkmate?
Son of Beast, 66.45 m (218 feet)
http://www.ultimaterollercoaster.com/coasters/records/wood_records.shtml#length

SECTION C
Animals

Dogs .... ***page 23***

1. Irish Wolfhound
   http://www.workingdogweb.com/DogFacts.htm
2. Saluki (probably)
   http://www.dogquotes.com/historyofdogs.htm
3. Basenji
   http://www.geocities.com/mycoconutmonkey/dog_longnshort.html
4. Chihuahua
   http://www.geocities.com/mycoconutmonkey/dog_longnshort.html
5. Greyhound
   http://www.geocities.com/mycoconutmonkey/dog_longnshort.html

Cats .... ***page 24***

1. (Siberian) Tiger
   http://www.dspace.dial.pipex.com/agarman/bco/fact1.htm
2. £ 25 000
   http://www.guinnessworldrecords.com
3. 16.5 cm
   http://www.guinnessworldrecords.com
4. Egyptian tomb, 300 000 cats
   http://www.catclub.net/cat_facts/worldrecord_details.cfm?id=17
5. 19–15 survived
   http://www.moggies.co.uk/html/records.html

Birds .... ***page 25***

1. Hummingbird
   http://www.victorialodging.com/birding/small_big_fast_slow.htm
2. Wandering Albatross
   http://www.victorialodging.com/birding/small_big_fast_slow.htm
3. Mallee Fowl
   http://www.earthlife.net/birds/intro.html
4. Ruppell's griffon (vulture)
   http://www.birding.com/BirdRecords1.htm
5. Ostrich
   http://www.arthropod.net/specimens/birds/egg.htm

Fish .... ***page 26***

1. Mekong giant catfish (Pla Beuk [disputed])
   http://www.geocities.com/buengsamran/home.htm
2. Whale shark
   http://www.buzzle.com/editorials/2-7-2004-50280.asp
3. Piranha
   http://www.extremescience.com/Piranha.htm
4. Ocean Sunfish
   http://artedi.fish.washington.edu/FishKey/mola.html
5. Stonefish
   http://www.saudidiving.com/dangerous-creatures.htm

Bears .... ***page 27***

1. Kodiak
   http://www.panda.org/news_facts/education/virtual_wildlife/animal_profiles/bear_brown.cfm
2. Sun Bear
   http://www.bagheera.com/inthewild/van_anim_sunbear.htm
3. Polar
   http://www.extremescience.com/PolarBear.htm
4. Spectacled
   http://www.thewildones.org/Animals/specBear.html
5. Giant panda
   http://www.enchantedlearning.com/subjects/mammals/panda/

Horses .... ***page 28***

1. Falabella
   http://www.studbook.co.za/society/miniature/min.htm
2. Arabian
   http://www.equinepost.com/resources/eps/epsViewArchive.asp?Archive=128
3. Thoroughbred
   http://www.horseshoez.com/breeds.html
4. Shire
   http://www.rarebreeds.co.nz/shire.html
5. Poitou
   http://www.infocenter.com.sv/poitou.htm

Snakes .... ***page 29***

1. Reticulated python
   http://www.planetark.com/dailynewsstory.cfm/newsid/23291/newsDate/31-Dec-2003/story.htm
2. Anaconda
   http://www.teach-at-home.com/fastfacts/animalkingdom/Records.asp
3. Taipan or Fierce Snake
   http://www.exn.ca/AustralianAnimals/fiercesnake.cfm
4. 33 feet
   http://www.news.bbc.co.uk/2/hi/asia-pacific/3354403.stm
5. Beaked Sea Snake
   http://www.manbir-online.com/htm2/snake.22.htm

Frogs .... ***page 30***

1. Poison Dart Frog
   http://www.shoarns.com/Frogs.html
2. 10.2 m (33 ft 5 ins)
   http://www.exploratorium.edu/frogs/mainstory/
3. Eleutherodactylus iberia / Gold Frog
   http://www.allaboutfrogs.org/weird/strange/small.html
4. Goliath
   http://www.allaboutfrogs.org/weird/strange/big.html
5. Australia
   http://www.allaboutfrogs.org/weird/strange/catholic.html

Great apes .... ***page 31***

1. Gorilla
   http://www.factmonster.com/spot/ape2.html
2. Bonobos
   http://www.factmonster.com/spot/ape2.html
3. Orang-Outang
   http://www.factmonster.com/spot/ape2.html
4. Orang-utan
   http://www.factmonster.com/spot/ape2.html
5. Smartest
   http://www.factmonster.com/spot/ape2.html

Rabbits .... ***page 32***

1. Flemish Giant
   http://www.geocities.com/Petsburgh/Haven/7837/Picking.html
2. Polish (Britannia Petite)
   http://www.centralpets.com/pages/critterpages/mammals/rabbits/RBT1439.shtml
3. True
   http://www.thebuffalohunter.com/rabbit%20meat.htm
4. English Lop
   http://www.vetcentric.com/magazine/magazineArticle.cfm?ARTICLEID=1715
5. Netherland Dwarf and Polish (Britannia Petite)
   http://www.houserabbit.co.uk/rwf/articles/polish_brit_petite.htm